Complicity

Books by Adam Sol

Jonah's Promise (2000)
Crowd of Sounds (2003)
Jeremiah, Ohio (2008)
Complicity (2014)

Complicity

poems

Adam Sol

McClelland & Stewart

Published simultaneously in the United States of America by McClelland & Stewart, a division of Random House of Canada Limited, P.O. Box 1030, Plattsburgh, New York 12901.

A cataloguing record for this publication is available from Library and Archives Canada and the Library of Congress.

ISBN 978-0-7710-7927-6

Printed and bound in Canada

McClelland & Stewart,
a division of Random House of Canada Limited
A Penguin Random House Company
One Toronto Street
Suite 300
Toronto, Ontario
M5C 2V6
www.randomhouse.ca

1 2 3 4 5   18 17 16 15 14

Contents

III

I

Dwarf

*I grew up with Pluto as a planet. And now I'm twenty-five, I turn around and
Pluto's no longer a planet. I gotta find that guy and elbow that guy in the nose.*
— Ron Artest, a.k.a. Metta World Peace

For one day I will not be ironic about the power of art.
For one day I will try not to be ironic about the power of art.

Tonight the President will use his best rhetoric
to make a case for more: more blood, more debt.

I will sit in my loveseat and wait for insight.
I will detect this insight by way of an inner ear organ
that knows – that believes it knows – insight when it hears it.

My inner ear likes the President's rhetoric: more effort, more death.
Sometimes it sounds like insight.
At other times it sounds like a man's voice in search of insight.

For me, for my inner ear,
the sound of this searching
is as close to insight as is usually available.

In other news, Pluto has been demoted to a dwarf planet
by the IAU's Working Group on the Definition of a Planet.

It has something to do with lopsidedness
and something to do with lack of influence:

"Bodies that dominate their neighborhoods 'sweep up'
asteroids, comets, and other debris, clearing a path along their orbits.
By contrast, Pluto's orbit is somewhat untidy."

And so the children weep because on their cartoon
maps of the solar system, Pluto the Ninth Planet
has been replaced with an unhappy face.
They write pleas to their congressmen, who can do nothing.

But today I have promised to stand by the claims of art,
to believe in things that,
while as far from the tables of power as Pluto is from Poughkeepsie,

to believe that they may have, that they may,
they may, they may, they may may may may.

Fire and desperation and hunger and belief. How to account for them?
How to measure their significations?
What can the cockeyed orbit of Pluto teach us about our earthly sufferings?

Chen Li wrote, "Traveling in the family of poetry
is the most substantial and warmest link
on the lonesome journey in the universe." If Mr. Li

wants to learn about loneliness, he should go to Pluto,
whose orbit extends to 7.4 billion kilometres from the sun,

and where there is no poetry,
though plenty is hurled hopefully up on its behalf.

It is a truism that, like a child, art has no
inherent use, and is often a draw on our resources.

As my grandfather once wrote, "Why do men write poems?
Why do men live?"

In those days, "men" meant "everyone,"
but recently the masculine general
has been declared a dwarf pronoun
by the IAU's Working Group on the Definition of Pronouns.

It will be a long winter on Pluto.
One hundred years, roughly.

Here it is the season of fallen fledglings.
They litter the sidewalks of this bulbous city,
some attracting flies,
some cheeping stupidly,
asking for help from parents
who understand the truth
and have begun their mourning rituals.
Sometimes storekeepers scoop the birds up
into shoeboxes and try to save them.

It's hard not to believe that Pluto
would be insulted by its recent reclassification as a dwarf,
which puts it on par with Eris, the Goddess of Discord.
Discord is only halfway to Hell, but it's also bigger.

Meanwhile art has been declared a dwarf pursuit
by the IAU's Working Group on the Definition of Pursuits.

No. I have promised.
We are moon-makers.
We take balls of ice
        and blow on them until
                they seem to hover and spin.
        Sometimes they achieve
an untidy presence
        that the President may refer to
                when he helplessly casts about –
more debt, more death –
                looking for a way to explain.

Pluto has three known moons:
Hydra, a monster.
Charon, the ferryman to oblivion.
And Nix, his mother, who *is* Oblivion.

Even Oblivion has an orbit.
        Even Oblivion bends the light.

Thinking About Thinking About Egypt

Earlier there was a windy ribbon
    flattering the screen

like a thing that should be evocative
    of something.

Then there was a pipe spewing ideas
    into the Gulf.

There were other things around
    also, if you

catch my meaning. Hey. Hey, what
    will you bring to the party,

chips or beer? OMG. Start with what
    you mean by "mean."

She wasn't angry, she was hurt. You know
    her son has lupus?

Sometimes when I say "mean," I mean
    "say," and sometimes

I mean "intend," even when intending
    doesn't mean anything.

On the other hand, meaningful things
    seem to be

happening in Egypt, old men kicking stones,
    refuting me thus,

young men throwing them. Don't say *présenter*
    when you mean *introduire*.

The riser insertion tube is certain to seal
    off the spillage.

But wait a second. We're trying to think
    entrepreneurially.

I'm talking about synergies. The clouds overhead
    are a property

you could procure and flip for twice
    the sell price.

Don't start on that again. Just wait until
    the Floridian

returns from his shift on the slick.

Op. 75, Sestina in B-flat for the Glockenspiel

In the empty classroom, at sunrise, a girl
sits on the floor, staring at a glockenspiel.
She's shredding the cuticles on her left hand
instead of starting to practise.
She doesn't want to play –
not yet, if ever. The irritating sound

of her teeth clicking is the only sound
in the band room. The cranky girl
has been dropped off early so she can play
a bit alone on the glockenspiel
before her classmates come to practise,
instrument cases clutched in their chapped hands

like luggage. They have such sure hands,
she thinks, and she can hear the sounds
they make, the laughter in the practise
rooms that make her feel like a little girl.
She is a "late bloomer," and like the glockenspiel,
she is awkward at the games they play.

Only it isn't really play,
is it? It's *life*. The boys put their hands
on the girls, who vibrate like glockenspiels,
with tinkling notes that sound
shrill and artificial to the girl.
But isn't this how it's always been practised?

And wouldn't she appreciate it more if she practised?
The ones who are good at it think of it as *play*.
That's what they think it means to be a girl.
But that's not me. I have ugly hands.
I don't know how to make the giggly sounds
they expect from me, except on the glockenspiel.

And what's the point of a glockenspiel
if I can't even concentrate and practise?
For some it's music, for others only sounds.
Now here come my bandmates, ready to play,
and all I've done is chew my hands
into bleeding mallets. I'm more stick than girl.

Practice begins, and it's time for the girl
to hoist her glockenspiel and exercise her hands.
Her imperfect self is on display. How does she sound?

Engagement

The young man knows he's going to die today, but he's wrong.
The other young man figures the army is the best way to improve his life,
      but he's wrong.
They both think their weapons will protect them, but they're wrong.
They both believe their prayers will help.

Their commanders have intentions and intelligence, but they're wrong.
We've heard the story before. It's wrong.
The news will document it, but it will be wrong.
The medium, the reception, the commentary, the commercial break.

The explosion will exceed the necessity of the occasion.
The exchange of fire will be unbalanced.
The response will be disproportionate.
The reporter is factually incorrect, morally misinformed.

The clear typeface and perfect binding are misleading.
The reader is uncomfortably and inappropriately implicated.
The tranquil mind is insufficient to the task.
The young men, necks dirty and damp, advance.

Before the Conference Call

Four minutes before the Conference Call,
this Something Unimportant day of July,
I am sitting in a stall with my smuggled
copy of poems by Paul Durcan,
thinking of Phil while someone on the other
side of the barrier, inches away,
hawks into a urinal. Oh, Phil,
I wish you were here with me now –
well, not exactly now, but at least on the Conference Call
because the voices will be strange and crackly,
and I am not certain I belong there, or even where
"there" is, if the District Manager
is in his car on the Cross Bronx Expressway
and the Sales Rep is in Trenton – which, as far as I know,
is Nowhere – and Legal is in Detroit but
not really Detroit, and I am in Desperate Straits.
I'd rather not be "there." I'd like to sit
some more and read Paul Durcan.
But it is time, already it is time,
and the poems will have to wait, and my
relief will have to wait . . . No!
I can be one minute late for the Conference Call.
Who would notice a minute, or two minutes?
"Sorry, I'm just logging on." *Oh, don't worry,
we're only getting started.* Yes, I will read
one more poem, I will wash my forlorn hands –
to hell with the Conference Call
and its insane demands! Phil, how you would
sneer to see me fumbling my way through,

but your sneering has always been an act of patronage.
You will not be on this Conference Call,
or on any other, ever again. Good, dead Phil.
But I will be. I will give productive input
with my fragrant hands slightly damp,
and my head full of hysterical Irishmen.
But first, "A Dublin Gynaecologist in Dubai."

Note Found in a Copy of A *Midsummer Night's Dream*

Lesley says she's going to write ya
        so I thought I'd say hello first!
I'm glad you two made up. You're a great guy
        and Lesley deserves the best. Well gotta go!
I love Jacob! Bye – Robyn.

Judging by the abrupt disappearance
        of highlighter, I'd guess
he gave up during Act Two. He? She?
        Did Bryan leave it here,
or was it never delivered?

Bryan,
        I did want to do
what we did last night! I just felt sick
        and like it would take all of my energy!
I did not do *anything that I did not* want *to do!*

Through the windows of the library
        the leaves shiver to the tune
of Max Bruch's *Scottish Fantasy.*
        It all tastes of the jammy fingers
that last handled these headphones.

Everything we did I wanted to happen!
        You didn't make me do anything!
If I didn't want to do something
        or didn't want you to do something
I would of said something to you about it!

It's the moment when Helena pursues
     Demetrius into the forest.
Use me but as your spaniel, spurn me, strike me,
     Neglect me, lose me; only give me leave,
Unworthy as I am, to follow you.

Evidence is emerging to suggest
     that Shakespeare's plays
may have been written by a sexually liberal
     daughter of Jewish musicians.
Bryan, I love you and I don't want you

to feel like you raped me! In the film,
     they're on bicycles,
and Calista Flockhart, perhaps surprisingly,
     holds her own.
I wonder if there's a cafeteria on this floor.

You DIDN'T so I wish you wouldn't feel that way!
     Barbara Johnson has an exceptional essay
on the usage of the second person address
     somewhere on these shelves.
I will not stay thy questions; let me go,

Or if thou follow me, do not believe
     But I shall do thee mischief in the wood.
Finally, here comes the rain.
     Even inside, the smell of hot pavement
gives the Reading Room an erotic humidity.

Have Akiko Suwanai's recordings
       of the *Fantasy* sold better than others'
because of the cover photo of her, lounging
       with her luscious hair raining down?
You are a pretentious patronizing dickwad.

Well, I have to go now and pay
       attention to Professor Roberts.
I Love You W/All My Heart!
       Her dotage now I do begin to pity.
Love Always, Lesley Anne Busch.

I could give this to Mike Roberts
       who might call the police
or at least a student counsellor.
       Not that it would change much.
Your wrongs do set a scandal on my sex.

How many wives have, on occasion,
       just lain back and let their men
get it over with? Probably all of them.
       How many men had the senses
to notice, and feel anger or guilt?

Fare thee well, nymph; ere he do leave this grove
       Thou shalt fly him,
and he shall seek thy love.
       And which would have been worse for them,
losing the note, or having someone return it?

Akiko Suwanai tears through the final runs of the *Fantasy*,
        her hands damp from the rain
that is peppering the library windows.
        Bottom, with his ass-head,
gropes his way toward the spellbound queen.

Security Camera

Sweethearts in school uniforms spoon froyo
    into each other's mouths on a bench across
        from the Korean consulate.
            Death to the infidels.

Down the street some boys shed their aprons
    to practise skateboard flops off an abandoned Buick.
        We shall bathe the streets in blood.
            Someone's mother drives by,

sipping bourbon from a spill-proof mug. The nose-ringed
    cashier says, "*Moulin Rouge* has layers
        that you miss unless you're on X."
            Revenge revenge revenge revenge.

A kid in an all-terrain stroller prefers his thumb
    to the pacifier strapped to his collar.
        Die, you fascist pig.
            Gravel gathers in the curb,

with stubs, shards, and other garbage.
    The bones of the filthy will burn forever.
        Little fists of grass muscle through the sidewalk cracks.
        The bus slows for an expectant mother,

but she's just catching her breath.
The godless will be torn to pieces by dogs,
and crows will gorge on their eyes.
A businesswoman in cowboy boots

fields a call between drags. There's blood in the water
and she's not going to miss her chance.

Security Review

Toronto, June 2010

We were concerned about an element
and wanted to protect the delegates
from injury or, worse, embarrassment.
And so we made arrangements and provisions,
allowed for some preventative suspensions
while, in secure rooms, members had discussions.
Outside there were confusions and concussions.
The logical next step is violence.
Luckily, logic wasn't in abundance.
Be thankful: cleanup in these circumstances
can involve notifying next of kin.
We'll just let the inquiries begin.
The outcome was that we preserved the peace.
We whored out our city, then fingered the receipts.

Tourist Town

Whatever Maple Marshmallow Fudge signifies,
we are receiving it, walking around

saying *ah!* to each other in our witty new T-shirts and caps.
We seek higher elevations in all currencies.

And *oh!* the landscape is *absolutely* authentic,
so when a woodpecker appears, as if on cue,

to diddle a charred spruce, we flock over
to record digital images. At night in our rented beds

we worry about what we've missed.
Did you set the PVR? Are these the experiences

we are imprinting on our children?
Is this what they will remember as their edenic youth?

Then let us show them scenic drives!
Let us sample the untainted local cuisine!

These are important tests! Anyone who has
a less-than-spectacular vacation will have one

less week off next year. Our online updates
must be characteristic and full of wonder!

Meanwhile, at home, our contraptions hunker patiently in their appropriate compartments.

An enterprising young rat has made his first foray into our pantry for a bite of Weetabix.

Wish You Were

We voted then and there to flee Tangiers
  and drive straight for Uranium.
The power steering went wonky, but the radio
  was a stream of good cheer.

Somewhere between Argyle and Angles
  we decided to build
a monument to monuments.
   It didn't turn out well.

After that we flew nonstop to Peshawar.
   The captain told us to prepare
for turbulence so we called our brokers
   and leveraged our investments.

Peshawar was about what we expected.
There was the usual blur of awe and horror.

From there I hitched to Quito
  on a school bus with neon undercarriage LEDs.
It took two months
  and three gallons of orange juice.

There were ibex speed-grazing the clouds.
  There were sad-mouthed women
with spectacular headdresses and accessories
  they had purchased online
from entrepreneurs in Cameroon.

The air smelled like a public pool.
The people spoke so many languages
they needed baskets to hold
all their words for fruit.

Reading Drew Faust at the Food Court

The human body is not like any other portion
of matter. A redhead aesthetician experiments

with a little extra pepper. Everything is available
to us here, even each other. The more we get used

to being killed, the more we like it. The staff,
diligent as they are, have not yet noticed

the tzatziki spattered on the ceiling. The sheer
number defied both administrative imagination

and logistical capacity. You have to ask for napkins,
but plasticware is plentiful and free. Nothing we

call trouble seems worth talking about. The Russian
girls don't mind if you look at their bare bellies,

but their boyfriends do. Our slogans are disputing
with each other across the pungent space. All we have

to do is lift a hand and we could pluck them right
out of the air. We are united in Styrofoam. And in

mild hunger, ruthlessly crushed without mercy.
I had no more feeling for him than if he had tripped

over a stump and fallen. When someone laughs,
everyone turns to see. Coca-Cola. Cold Harbor.

Manchu Wok. Deep, boys, deep, so the beasts
won't get me. Waste here, recycle there.

That new kid really knows how to skewer a chicken.
I was kind of hungry, and got used to the pretty sights.

The Last Matador

It is good to be finished, finally.
I am relieved. The protesters
and politicians have their points,
and if a certain species of man
is allowed to fade into extinction
we should, perhaps, praise progress
and look for new sources of spectacle.

Man will have his bloody games.
Just not this one. It is a pity,
but only for those of us who believe it
to be a form of art.

My fellow killers have changed
their names and entered
the banking industry. We are too
decorous for soldiering, though
one or two have found a place
with the drug lords, who still
feel that death and style belong together.

I will miss the adulation, I won't
deny it – the roses they threw. Blood
on the sand, sand on the roses. But mostly
I will miss my body's lithe movement
alongside the beast, and his magnificent heat.
And the moment when he looks
at me, the banderillas draped

over his back like the feathers of an exotic bird,
when he looks at me with that
single-minded resigned ferocity
as if to say, *So, it will be you.*

Consequences

First a mule knocked on our door
          asking for a cup of sugar
and perhaps some non-dairy creamer.

Then the piano fell over, laughing
          at a joke my mother told.
The grass grew orange and blue.

Next we went to war, tra la,
          and a local boy's
kidneys were turned into a stew.

Our truck could not turn left
          so we betrayed our neighbours
and played brave games at dusk.

A parade of far-fetched promises
          barely held its own
in wrestling matches against the market.

Meanwhile a magpie plotted against
          the stars with charts
she stole from us, but we didn't mind,

because we were cutting the spruce
          for a scaffold.
We sang minor songs of antipathy

and someone's black-eyed sister tied
        a double-knot out
of an octopus. We were the first

of our kind to witness all this.
        We were pioneers of experience.
This made us feel lucky and proud.

Water Language

I wanted to walk to Waukegan,
      but the road was like an oboe reed.

I wanted to break bread with Esau
      but found only rotten fruit.

I wanted to make myself a magical musician,
      but the waters came,

and my skin has split. I am a broken drum.

Where can I dig out my hollow, now
      that my legs are bowed with mud?

And how can I set up my blind behind the pines,
      now that rain has torn from me my spirit, as a hiker tears a web?

Where once were spiritual mysteries, now
      I see a wide expanse of bog.

I slam mosquitoes by the gross against my calves,
      and the blood is brilliant. It is my own.

Once I wanted to feather the field with letters to lovers and men,

and instead I have strung this contraption together
      with loose strands from the carpet

and tree sap, seeped to repel beetles.
　　Now, friends, wet needles, splayed out

to shed your water, tell me how to begin again
　　with this bruised shoe I call my mouth.

II

Trial Notes

I was in movies and commercials.
There is proof of me in posters.

People are nostalgic
for the man I used to seem.

Our judge is a just judge.
Our just judge is just a judge.

The men outside would prefer
this went on a little longer.

The chair is a chair.
The desk is a desk.
The desk is also sometimes a chair.

Disaster Contest

There were reams of testimony to be sorted through. The judges were underpaid, desperate for the cash to pay back well-meaning but burdensome loans from friends and family. We scanned the pages trying to discover the secrets of our rivals. Was that my schoolmate who lost a child in the river? Didn't she spend a summer in Cincinnati? The names had been removed, but we had our suspicions and hopes. The Holocaust memoirs and slave diaries were straightforward, but the tales of exile, earthquake, and torture were hard to indentify, the names so general and the experiences and feelings ultimately so common. One couldn't even trust rape victims to be women, something last year's judges had learned to their embarrassment.

Still, we were up to the task, discarding the painful, the sad, and the ironic in favour of the gut-wrenching, the tragic, and the horrific: the lives broken on a national scale, tales from vanishing peoples, environmental catastrophes so severe as to warp genetics for generations. Is the rape of a woman as a part of a systematic humiliation of an ethnic group more or less disastrous than the rape of a woman by her own father? Was forcing a man to cook and eat his own hand more profound because it had very possibly never been done before? Was simple murder obsolete? Was war?

But now that the contest was gaining international attention, there was a spirit of one-upmanship that had not been anticipated. Arguments broke out in the print media, with surprising dismissals of some of the contestants' pain and suffering. Increasingly the organizers were concerned that rather than serve as a purgative, the contest might be heightening the public's, to say nothing of the perpetrators', taste for disaster. Was it conceivable, as had been rumoured, that victims might dare or even *encourage* their tormentors to take their cruelties to another level for the sake of the potential reward from the Contest? Could the tables then be turned and a torturer submit an entry based on the shame and public ignominy incurred following the successful candidacy of one of the man's own victims, or by the extraordinary pressure placed on him by superiors or even by his charges for the dubious honour of being included on next year's shortlist? Could one of *us* submit a memoir of the psychological trauma resulting from the experience of reading about, or perhaps contributing to, all of these disasters? Each year there were more and more entries.

We Oppose the Teaching of Higher Order Thinking Skills

I've been reading Bill Matthews
remembering a visit he made
to Indiana and I played a waltz
and my classmates danced. I think
he hit on someone but that may
have just been my envy. I love
the way his poems inhabit his life
which is something mine are not
allowed to do – the way he starts
a poem, "What did I think . . ."
or "I've been reading Bill Matthews . . ."
He could do that in the early '80s.
Now nobody thinks. Even
the Texas Republican Party platform
agrees with me, though for them
it's *shouldn't* and for me it's *can't*.
Boyo, Facebook went into a feeding
frenzy over that one. We were all,
I think, overreacting to a misinterpretation.
Matthews would have liked Facebook,
but probably YouTube more,
because of all the vintage recordings
of jazz greats you can find if you
can spell their names. Art Tatum
tearing through Chopin's Waltz
in C-sharp Minor, holy shit. I'm just
saying. K just about buried himself
in the sound of all that unmaking
though when I talk to him he seems

fine. He takes his kid to the dentist
just like a citizen. Me, I'm out here
on the metaphorical porch swing
looking for other ways to speak.
And Bill Matthews is long gone,
before YouTube or anything.

Check Authenticity Here

1

      "The quotes in question
were intentional misquotations
or improper combinations
or did not exist.
But my motives were pure. I insist."
      – Jonah Lehrer, roughly.
Meanwhile Joaquin Phoenix gruffly
renders his 2012 apology
to Letterman for trying to seem
like a man trying not to seem
deranged. Psychology
and PR are dating again.
It is the age of *Homo praetendens*.

2

Trying to write a normal
poem I keep writing "Metacicada"
instead of "Magicicada,"
as if part of me
would prefer a self-referential periodical
hemiptera to one that's supernatural.
Seventeen years growing underground
then four weeks screeching in a tree.
We are all, sadly, bound
to live out our re-enactments.
Even Ben Lerner's fraudulence
is fraudulent, but at least
it isn't plagiarized. Mostly.
This last line should come as a surprise.

3

Joaquin wasn't really high
in February '09,
though he did gain the weight.
For a year he pretended to be
a total asshole straight
out of his own publicity.
These are the tasks of art.
To fake it until faking
is its own kind of making.
Try not to be too smart.
Lord Black enjoys some spreadable
cheese-flavoured food
while arguing his case for good
behaviour. It's edible.

4

"It is still not known
whether he killed himself, or went to Mexico."
What's the diff?
The man that was Weldon Kees
is dead if no one sees
him and gives a shit.
The prep needed to execute
a disappearance is overblown:
just stop tweeting,
your language life receding
into a server's archive
where only Kenny Goldsmith
can delightfully mine
it for meaning's opposite.

5

The problem with inauthenticity
is that it's hard to feel for very long.
There is, then, room for virtuosity.

If you can play, you can pretend
your instrument is broken,
but the opposite isn't true:

Letterman could seem right through
the schmuck. And Colbert can't
fake his love for the applause.

When Jake Shimabukuro plays "Hallelujah"
on his custom ukulele all of YouTube
rejoices in his imitation of the song.

Don't we? There's scant
evidence but plenty of laws.

6

Here's what I learned about *Magicicada*
from the experts at Wikipedia:

When it emerges from the earth
the nymph climbs to a decent perch

and performs its final moult online.
All that lost and lonely time

it spent underground gnawing the roots of trees
like a teenager without an email address

has culminated in this vulnerability –
its flesh pale, raw, and digitally undressed.

Soon it will harden and join the throng
in the "chorus tree" trying to entice
an original spin on a traditional song,
but for now its exposure will have to suffice.

7

These amusements notwithstanding
I refuse to give up trying
to be a person searching for understanding.
Why do you think I'm lying?

To resist the throwing up of the hands.
To imagine a world of things that matter.
To pass through these shatterings
with something intact. And Sandy

tears up Cuba and Atlantic City
like a pissed-off reality
show girlfriend, as if part of the reason
for her fury is the previews for next season –

otherwise, why all the drama?
To storm bigger than Romney v. Obama.

8

Dear Snooki, we too
strive for virtue
and in our seats
while we watch you
shake to beats
we cannot hear
we yearn to be nearer,
to see you more clearly,
love you more dearly,
the way the aspirants to heaven
did in *Godspell* with major sevenths.
Vigilant, flexible, may your boy Lorenzo
learn to mimic the cartoon in cameos
but resemble himself outside the studio.

9

Finish this. It is not what I expected.
        Soon it won't even be fun.
I am confused and conflicted,
        and worried for my sons.
It's hard to invent a personality

that doesn't make me feel like an ass.
        But soon this will pass.
My exoskeleton will harden
        and I'll resume with the jargon
that reflects my complicity.

Until then, play me the ukulele
        version of "Bohemian Rhapsody."
Are those the real words, or are they just fantasy?
        Search me.

Template Poem

Here I am at the specific location,
with its world-infected familiarity,
and its overlooked, unlikely beauty. It is here
where, after a brief meditation on an esoteric topic,
I will come to a realization at once profound
and elementary, something we all know
that had never before achieved itself in song.
How exposed I am, here in these words,
translating my insights into language both elaborate
and brutal. And how hopeful of you
to press on despite the odds,
the paltry expense and frequent disappointments.
But this isn't about you. You sit down.
This is about truth as our attentions
drift to a seemingly unrelated tidbit,
the average number of molecules in the width of a human hair,
or something funny Bob Dylan once said in Tucson.
Off on tangents we worry together how I will pull off the conceit,
but you can see it in your peripheral vision:
the end of the poem approaching
like the end of a moving walkway at Lester B. Pearson Airport.
Your gate is behind you now, but the glide
of each well-constructed sentence
brings us closer to our anticipated departure.
Now the metaphor begins to collapse (where are we off to?),
and the model threatens to devolve into parody.
You have wasted your time when you could have
exercised your logical mind solving sudoku.
Don't worry. It's almost over. Congratulate yourself

for reading the poem. Your judgments of its merits
are informed by a whole host of criteria
that few have access to. The world is full
of cretins who don't read poems, but you
are not among them. You are vastly
superior in many respects.
It turns out this poem is about you after all!
You are a species no less endangered or precious
than the narwhal. The unacknowledged legislators of our world,
as everyone knows, are actuaries,
but who needs legislation,
or the world for that matter,
when we can huddle together at the end of the poem,
relishing our rarified pleasures?

Four Theatricals

1. *Coming of Age Story*

Stage Right two girls are playing jacks in cute summer dresses, knee-highs, and patent leathers. They sing quietly. Stage Left a third girl, same age, dressed same, with an old Taiwanese man in a hospital gown. He lies on the floor, silent, back to the audience, right arm raised. She is beating him with a laptop computer.

In a short while, one of the girls Stage Right appears to win. The loser sighs, rises, and walks Left to the others.

LOSER: (to girl with computer) Your turn.

Girl gives the laptop to the loser and treads Right to play jacks. The loser begins beating the old man, who makes no sound or movement.

2. *Situation Comedy*

MARTIN enters Stage Right wearing a raincoat. Applause of recognition. He remarks perfunctorily on the weather, makes as if to remove the coat, then notices a YOUNG BLACK MAN seated on the easy chair Down Left. The YOUNG BLACK MAN is smoking a cigarette, facing out, and is unaware of Martin's presence. Something is deeply concerning him. He wears blue-grey trousers and a green bowling shirt with the name "Calhoun" stitched over the left pocket. Martin, coat unbuttoned but not removed (beneath, his suit is rumpled), slowly works his way Down and Left, approaching the YOUNG BLACK MAN and staring intently at him.

His hands have instinctively risen to shoulder level, as if he is about to shove something, or deflect a blow.

When Martin reaches Centre, the YOUNG BLACK MAN calmly turns and notices him. He looks Martin up and down and takes a brief tug at his cigarette. Martin has stopped moving. He scarcely blinks. The YOUNG BLACK MAN stands up – he is a bit taller than Martin – and leans over to stub out his cigarette in an ashtray on a small table next to the easy chair. He briefly rubs his thumb and forefinger together as if to remove the smell of nicotine, then turns to face Martin.

Canned laughter.

3. *Farce*

A sidewalk café. Perfect weather, genteel patrons sipping cappuccinos and nibbling pastries. A mime entertains us, climbing invisible walls, tripping over phantom pets, etc. The audience largely ignores him until he imitates the walk of an elderly passerby, earning him his first big laugh. It occurs to him that this is his gift. He pretends to kick two lovers and the response is full-throated.

A young woman in a summer dress enters and crosses Upstage, past the mime. Her head is down, hair hiding her face. The mime follows, mincing. The patrons chuckle approvingly.

She has almost reached Upstage Left exit when he startles her with a flourishing tip of his cap. The flinch in her shoulders makes the crowd roar, but suddenly he's stopped. Something in her face we can't make out. Our utensils clink. He clears his throat. She grasps his gloved hand.

4. *Musical*

Curtain. Two smiling, chubby friends in zoot suits come forward as
if about to sing. Suddenly a scream from the audience, a shot, and a
woman crying, "Charlie, what have you done?!" The actors seat them-
selves on the edge of the stage, still smiling, and watch as the audience
erupts and rumbles like bay waters. From outside the theatre come
sirens, on key.

We Are Here

We are here because Amanda asked.
We are here in turquoise and sand.
We are here to help.

We are here at the corner of Sheppard and Bathurst.
We are here every Tuesday and Thursday.
We are here up to our necks.

We are here to save the day.
We are here to impale ourselves on the pike of love.
We are here to spite our mothers.

We are here because of a series of spectacular chemical accidents.
We are here despite ontological doubt, *because* of ontological doubt.
We are here with ontological doubt.

There is a here there and a there there. Even in Oakland.
We'd prefer to be there, but then there would be here.
We are here because the tickets were on sale.

We are here to do God's will.
We are here to throw ourselves at the sheik's mercy.
We are here to kick some Alabama ass.

We are here in the library, reading difficult books.
We are here with our hands in our hats.
We are here, but we cannot see you.

We are here in the middle of a sentence. No, near the end.
We are here, with no Coca-Cola in sight.
We are here exhausted, with so much more to do.

You Have Been Awarded a Fellowship in Synaesthesia

Here is the bench where we sat eating
artificially flavoured dairy products,
waiting for news. How a disembodied
voice can say things and set the world to orange.
Complications. Congratulations. Casual.
Casualties. Here is a crushed sandwich.
Here is a rancid dog. Here is my mother's
lip mole. The cool kids are bobbing their heads
to *Pigeon* and Evan Penny. Two hours
of entrancing distraction, smoked
turkey and tomato on rye. Those discs
were found in a lingerie store drawer. Play
track 12 from 32C. What I mean
when I say *Hm* is something like what Harriet
means when she says, *Indigenous species at risk*.
If the underdog wins too often he'll lose
himself. When I was a boy I used to imagine
an old man chanting. When I was a girl
it was a garlic piano. These noodles
want to flick your chin with splash. Is that a scar
or should we worry? We must resist the urge
to throw up our hands like a pizza man.
No one knows when the game ends. Or how
to score. Or why we're playing. I win.

Day's Work

Yesterday I buried my foreskin in a corner
of the football field, where orange rinds
and spat juice have made the earth a fragrant paste.

The oozing has ebbed. I have been able
to remove the gauze and walk
like something remembering how to be a man.

So this morning I went to watch my shackled uncle
chew his gums at the spastic cafeteria.
All the attendants have tattoos of eyes on their eyelids.

They were despairing over who would tally our scores
now that the Commissioner has been commissioned.
Will Troy be a C or must Tyson suffice?

When I returned my tray, all the forks
were milk, the spoons meat.
Poor uncle: nothing can save him

from living out the rest of his life as himself.
I limped to the streetcar
for my class in standard Mandarin.

Our Esteemed Teacher uses Italian curses
to illustrate his lessons
and my classmates trade prescriptions and threats.

I cross my knees, listening for the peculiar grammar.

Morning Song

Every morning at ten
the man with no hands
orders his hamburger

and kicks a chair back
to watch the pavement
crack. Someone lashed

her retriever to the streetcar.
The assistant manager
is explaining product

placement to her inferiors.
What do you know? What
do you need to know?

In comes the boy
from the bank, his chin
stained red. Who says

we must prepare
for the worst? Out back,
the baker's boy

bears down on his pedals,
calves bunched
like a pair of peaches.

Off he goes,
trailing the humiliating
smells of bread and hope.

They Will Take My Island

You taught me language, and my profit on't
Is I know how to curse.

They will take my island
        if I don't scorch it down to cinders, though
                to speak truly,

I did not know it was an island
        until they said so.
                I thought it was the world.

The river-fish would drift
        into my clasp and I would gnaw
                on their flesh while the gills still

gasped. It had edges and pleasures
        and dangers.
                What more is a world?

Then they arrived with their instruments.
        They taught me so much
                about my home it became

strange as my body became strange
        when it bloomed.
                They renamed

the birds after their own birds.
They taught me to sing for them,
and to delight in singing for them.

I watched their plots evolve
as a monkey watches
a jaguar wrestle a snake.

Then one day they gathered on the sand,
and my princess held the hand
of a young god,

and I cursed myself for a fool,
and the drunk bowed his head
and a pig was cooked,

and even I was given
a piece of hoof to suck on.
They sang a song

and climbed onto some felled trees
and sailed away to heaven,
leaving me

to the wordless noises. I returned
to my caves and corners
but couldn't remember

what to hide from. The jaguars
        had been slaughtered.
                The fish tasted raw.

I sat on a stone
        and tried to imagine
                what to think of myself.

                They will return.
        How can they not return
if they spoke of this place so enchantingly?

                And how can I not try
        to prevent them, now that
I know it is mine? How can I not resist

                with my very teeth,
        or enact my revenge
with immolation? Every sunset

                I ascend the heights
        of my puny kingdom,
and scan the sea for sails.

Evening Song

My son, sleeping,
pulls a phone book
onto his chest.
His breath slowly
settles to a wheeze.

Tuesday night.
After my shift,
I've got the whole
bus ride home to
decide if I should live.

Laundry panic.
Phone bill panic.
Anger panic.
Television.
A new scar on my arm.

If I'd known
that this would be
my life, I would
have killed someone
before I lost my nerve.

No, that's not true.
I don't know
what I would have done.
Twelve more lights
then 257 sidewalk squares

till home. My boy
tries to turn
onto his side
to relieve the
pressure. Can't.

That Year's Fall

Then one night your wife wakes you by falling into the piano
the cheerful chime of a D suspended second
resounds around the house as you hurl
yourself to her sliding in your socks what is it what's
wrong you crouch beside her on the hardwood
prepared to clear the airway call 911 breathe
into her mouth pound her chest or who knows cut a hole into her
  blocked throat
but a part of your mind suspended over the tableau
is thinking not what's happening but oh
so this is how it happens
this is how crisis will come to us
you have been waiting your whole lives together
asking the question and now there's relief in encountering the answer
but no she's just feverish and dizzy disoriented
from the Benadryl and wants to sleep a while
with her cheek on the cool sustain pedal her breath
like stale soup and her eyes squeezed shut
against the bathroom light she'd left on
so all you can do is bring water and flip the switch
bring a blanket and grope back to bed with the questions
unanswered but fully awakened now who how
intermittent cars whirr past the house
you can hardly bear the interval between

Nearly Blank Calendar

Her husband, needing a change,
      accepts the spoon
of pudding she nudges
      past his teeth.
Butterscotch. His surprised eyes.
      Some dribbles
from his chin onto his lap.
      The pants
are forty years old and shiny
      at the knee.

     *

Step 2: Starting with
      the fingers
and working your way
      to the armpit,
wash and rinse one arm,
      dry it
with a warm towel, and
      cover it with
a blanket.

     *

The face, its expressions
        are so changed,
it's easy to see he's not
        the man she –
but the hands, the wrists,
        the arms are
the same. The burned hair
        smell. Don't
talk about that. Leave that alone.

        *

A nearly blank calendar
        on the nightstand.
No appointments in April.
        May 4: Throat
Test. May 5: Pay ConEd.
        May 6: Dr.
Dandi refer to OncGastro.
        May 15: Philharmonic,
in pencil, crossed out in pen.

        *

Step 3: Remove bedclothes
        down to the patient's
waist. Wash and dry the chest
        and abdomen.

Cover the patient
        with a warm towel
or blanket as soon as his
        chest is clean.

        *

Leave that out. What would
        you want
to tell a story like that for?
        Leave that out.
At Schroon Lake there
        was an Italian boy
I let kiss me under a pine
        tree. Sap
on my new blue blouse.

        *

Tip. Nail. Pad. Print.
        Cuticle. Knuckle.
Distal Phalanx. Middle Phalanx.
        Proximal Phalanx.
Thumb. Index. Middle. Ring.
        Small. Life Line.
Love Line. Health Line. Palm.
        Thenar. Hypothenar.
Metacarpals. Carpals. Wrist.

*

This is the story you want
            to tell your
literary friends about me?
            It's not my
business but I think you
            could have made
a more interesting choice.
            Tell about
my father giving an Astor
            credit
at the Gristede's he managed.
            I kept the books
for him after school, and
            I know
she never paid up. Tell
            about how
I slept for years under
            a piano.

*

Boiled water. Rinsed skillet.
            Clean sheets.
Leftover oatmeal. Aching legs.
            Pill case. Tissue.
Radio. Gave up hope. Breakfast.
            Two hours' sleep.

Stop it. Don't ask me more.
    When I'm dead
and you're sorting through the house,
        you can keep
the calendar, for all the good it'll do you.
    They give them
out at the bank for free.

            *

She would plant a heel
        on the base
of the sewing machine to lever
        him sideways
so she could sponge
        the bedsores
on his shoulders. How he
        would wince
and shiver. Don't say that.

            *

I met a woman once who
        dated Hemingway.
Her name was Irene.
        They played tennis.
She had all these letters.
        You know

what she did with them? When
        the biographers
came calling, she *burned* them,
        that's what she did,
all but one.
        Which she framed.

III

What I Know About Phenomenology

Rock Smash is a better attack against normal types
but Seismic Toss does more damage against higher levels.

Summer 1989: the grapes in Burgundy and the corn in Iowa
are just beginning to swell. The Beastie Boys launch
Paul's Boutique and Tiananmen Square is transforming
from a place to an event. *They tell us what to do?*
Hell, no! Shadrach, Meshach, Abednego. All around people
doing things – illegal things – that would burn images
and soundscapes into our minds forever.

I say "our" with some hope. Also "forever."
People have been playing the flute for at least forty thousand years.
The oldest we have was made from a mammoth tusk.

As I get older, and my vision of my potential
fades into the disappointment of my self, how do
I continue to strive for the things I know
are either beyond my capacity
or beneath my contempt?

Eventually, two men dressed as medics came
and escorted Tank Man straight to oblivion.
No, that's not right. Whoever he is,
I've seen him graffitied on walls from Cobán to Benghazi.

You will gain more experience
if you apply the maximum power-up.

The Gladiator

When they conquered my city, I hated them
for their strategy. How else could their gang
of debtors, ruffians, programmers, and mercenaries
lay waste to a thousand years?
We flailed against their formations
like ducks against a screen.

But now, half starved, half lame
from our lost last defence,
and still in shock from my shackles,
I recognize that I am nothing beside them.
There is no secret trick to victory
against these monsters. Our faith and factories

did nothing to prepare me for their well-fed bodies,
any one of which will make
quick work of me as soon as the gate lifts.
I'd fare better against the lions.
Prince that I am – that I was –
I am not even fit for their great arenas,

but must die here in this half-filled provincial park,
training grounds for the up-and-comers of their profession.
I can hear the locals outside,
bored suburbanites, crackling their delicacies,
stacking their apple cores and spitting
into Styrofoam cups. The women flirt and the men

respond. Oh, I was misled by our epics,
our anthems and blogs.
I believed that our stories would save us
from their magnificent efficiency. But how could I not?
My people were composing multimedia cantatas
while theirs were struggling with agriculture.

My fathers understood the tectonic tremors of the earth
while theirs merely dug into it, like prairie dogs.
They once looked to us for guidance and succor,
and now here am I,
pissing myself like the boy in the movie,
while we wait for the signal.

In front of me is the smell of what a man must become
if he is to survive until sunset.
What good are my oils and perfumes, my shampoos and astringents?
Look at his deltoid pulsing while he grips his weapon.
He needs no elliptical machine,
not when there are patsies like me to keep him bloody and in trim.

My people are scattered,
my family lost,
my lands distributed,
my electronics smashed.
What is left for me but to choose a death
that is noble like Kenobi's or heroic like the Sundance Kid's?

Now the commercial interlude has ended.
The gate cranks open.
I am the dust of the earth,
and the sun is a glorious vacuum cleaner.
Lord, save me in the archives.
Replay the beats of my people in infinite loop.

Magicicada

Don't call
their seventeen

nymphal years
dormant.

That's a *life*,
and the six

weeks of noisy
flight and

hormonal whirr
are just

a confusing,
ecstatic,

and ultimately
painful

transition back
underground.

Poem for Noah Pozner

He died, in part,
from a bullet to the face
that obliterated his jaw.

*

That is what the article reported.

*

We must teach our children
to be afraid. We must
teach them *not* to be afraid.

*

The uses of the occasion. The positioning.
What if he had been a black boy, etc.
Wayne LaPierre didn't shoot those children.
The rage of reaching through the screen
and being bounced back.

*

Hugging his mother with his shirt off
"so I can feel your heart better."

*

A short private life. A public death.
Newsmen and politicians and poets doing their damned
best to understand what you mean.

*

The smiling photos have nothing
to do with everything.

*

Twenty-one thousand children
die every average day.

*

What only poetry can confront.
Not adequately, but closer to it
than anything else at our disposal.

*

Not just the horror and sadness,
but also the anger and paralysis,
the curiosity and confusion,
the relief and nausea,

*

and how the national consciousness focuses
then dissipates: crises in Cyprus,
Syria's exploding schoolhouses, teenage rape
victims hanging themselves in yellow bedrooms,
the Boston Marathon.

*

His twin survived. May she live
safely in our world
and perhaps even raise a son in your name.

*

This is a prism. When light shoots through, all of its pieces come apart
into different colours. Did you know that light was made up of colours?
When they strike a mirror, you only see the light. But when they pass
through the prism, you can see what the light is made of.

*

I just
want people to
know the ugliness
of it so we
don't talk about it
abstractly, like
these little

angels just
went to heaven. No.
They were
butchered.

City Song

Who's seen the phantom boy
        who used to drum pennies against metal gratings
                down here by the switching station?

Where could he be, now that I finally
        have something to show him,
                after months of marching past

on my way to strategy meetings and lunches?
        I used to shrug
                at his pathetic entreaties,

suggesting that I had nothing to give him that day,
        not today,
                and the shrug satisfied both of us.

He would smile and say, "Nice day," or "Cold one,"
        and I would take that for
                a metaphysical forgiveness.

In this way we achieved an understanding,
        a sort of communion between men,
                an agreement to accept

that we would never touch each other.
        But here I am,
                I have walked this strip of sidewalk

for two hours in search of him
because I think I found his dog behind my building,
half buried in leaf oatmeal.

Bones so thin they could be syringes.

Ivory Fugue

From her own flesh, Parvati sculpted him
to guard the door while she bathed
so she wouldn't be disturbed by her husband's
crass henchmen.
Ganesh, Remover of Obstacles.

*

Learning a fugue at fourteen. Ducking under on a tricky turn,
my thumb caught

the lip of a key and flipped off the cover. Enamel scallop,
with a grain like hewn wood.

We slathered carpenter's glue to repair it, but the split piece
curled up from the key,

so we replaced it with plastic: flat white with no feature.

*

First, kill the elephant.
Machine guns work
but poisoned watermelons
are best for avoiding
rangers. Then use
a hacksaw to extract
the twelve-pound tooth
from its socket in the cheek.

A warm wet spring and out pop
    the tank tops.
The grade elevens are skipping physics,
    pursing their lips
over sweet iced frappés. Their oily
    shoulders glisten.
Fitness club posters urge us to look
    better naked.
Blasts of pastel fleshtones evoke
    the standard
responses. The barista's collarbone
    churns
as she pumps liquid sweetener into
    a plastic cup.

*

Such hazard now must doting Tarquin make
Pawning his honour to obtain his lust.

*

Some say he lost the tusk in a fight
    with Parashurama.
Others that he removed it himself
    to use as a pen
while transcribing a great epic poem
    by Viasa.

*

Over the last ten years
men have harvested
half of Africa's elephants
to supply the rich raw
material for the greatest
carvers in the world.
He said, "I don't see
the elephant. I see the Lord."

*

Babe, your boobs
are like light bulbs
> *not the new energy savers*
> *but those old-school incandescents.*

They're like those
upside-down question marks
> *the Spanish put before questions.*

I'm saying the shape
does something to me, honey,
> *and I want to put my hands on them.*

Or maybe
if you'd just let me
     stare a while from my end of the lab?

*

The artist kept the window open
     so her nipples would remain
          erect in the cool air
               even when it began to rain.
               Standing Odalisque in a Red Window.

*

FUGITIVE WARLORD
POACHES ELEPHANTS
TO FUND REBELLION
VS. GENOCIDAL TYRANT

*

At the next table: adulterous rendezvous
disguised as a business proposition.
     Or vice versa.

When she laughs, she leans forward
with her chin raised, exposing the landscape
of her neck and chin to his appreciative view.

*

The exquisite peg box of a nineteenth-century
viola da gamba
still retains the sloped curve of the animal.

*

Behold thou art fair, my love,
and the world is dimmed by your light.
Your skin is as the sky on a spring day:
clear and without blemish.

Your breasts are nectarines, sweet to taste,
and your hair is fragrant and lush.
Syrup drips from your tongue, and your lips
are as soft as a breeze through a willow.

How your eyes encircle me.
How they delve into my soul!
Your hips curve like a cello.
I will encircle you with my thighs
and make music with my hands between.
Let me hear you sing.

*

His hand that yet remains upon her breast –
Rude ram, to batter such an ivory wall!

*

Cutie gets used
Small tit milf ass rammed
Beautiful teen ravished
Biker babe shredded
Pound that pussy
Cunt punished
Ass plastered

*

Behind a tree the boy crouches, gazes
into the middle distance, holding his father's blade.

If the creature wanders too far then all will be lost.
But if things go well, his efforts will be worth

three months' grain for his family,
and perhaps a wife.

*

Ganesh, Patron of the Arts,
whose curved trunk and great body showers blessings,
kindly remove all obstacles from our endeavours.
Illuminate our minds with wisdom.
Fill us with righteous judgment
as we lay our confusion at your holy feet.

Sally Hemings

At times I pity your desire,
fleeting as it is, hemmed in
by honour on the one side,
your failing frame on the other.

At other times I fear it, for how
it can spin such a clear mind
away from ideas that seem
so much larger and more lasting.

But of course nothing
is more lasting than the kind
of desire you have for me.
Except the need to make it pure.

Resisting the Urge to Resist Pathetic Fallacy

Almost the sky breaking apart
into sentiment. Almost the slippage,
the pretend, the letting myself
fall back into the metaphorical pool.
You stood there on the balcony,
looking out over the smog-smeared town,
and something inside me moved
around, responding. There was a sudden
breeze through the window that was
so full of humidity and immanence
it seemed to presage your turning
around and coming back to bed.
And then you did,
and we were in the familiar territory
of each other's bodies while the first
pungent thuds came careening
to the concrete. The barometer
cooperated, we took a delicious
slow morning and your rising breaths
were met with equal power by the storm.
How the rich rain came down,
and how we attuned ourselves
to its progress, listening and answering
the way jazz musicians do. Except
we were each other's instruments,
inexpertly played, imperfectly made,
and no less pleasure regardless. It *did*
rain for us that morning in B_____.
For us it did rain. Out on the street

the well-meaning citizens did their best
not to hurt anyone, and now,
remembering it I can feel the mind
straining. So end it here, before
the conceit breaks down, and I recall
anything else that happened that day
in B_____, the excess acts and texts,
the argument over the price of a meal,
and traditions that threaten to collapse
the morning under a different pressure,
the impending light already
leaking onto the matted
carpet and soiling the Remind
me how I still love you
and let the rain rain its ludicrous rain.

Toward an Idea of Citizenship

I'm trying not to think of my country as a girl
      drinking coffee in a drizzle

after her boyfriend has gotten on the train.
      Her dyed-black hair

is piled on her head, this morning's cobbling together
      of last night's style and fire.

Her eyeliner is smudged, but not from crying.
      She sips from the cup,

thin shoulders folded under the boy's windbreaker.
      She's got work in an hour –

Saturday's bleary-eyed afternoon shift better
      than jealous Friday night's.

She'll have time at the register to wonder
      if what she's so sad about

is him going or just knowing what comes next.

There is always a girl saying goodbye
      to a boy who is leaving

the shitbin they call home. She is always
      wondering if he will return,

if he will send for her, if she will be stuck
        her whole life

while he goes on to become a partner in some firm
        and father brilliant children

with a woman from the city whose father
        did the same thing forty years ago.

There are always the women in the city
        who know the names of artists

and designers and have elaborate ambitions
        instead of impulses and regrets.

And there is always the boy,
        who is blank with the change,

whose only chance is to forget everything,
        who hates the town

for being so familiar, who hates the girl for staying
        and himself for leaving,

who hates the train, the sky, his oily face, the traces
        of kisses on his neck,

and most of all the insistent pulse that pushes him
toward whatever it is

in this forsaken world he is going to become.

Watching Jack Layton's Funeral with the Kids While Recovering from Wisdom Tooth Extraction

Corpus, a body. Tonguing its wounds. The idea that the TV is a distraction from pain. The budget crisis. Percocet prohibits reading the paper. The almost comforting taste of blood. Reports of robocalls. Vanilla pudding. Strands of stitching in the gums. I remember, a few months ago, wondering if the shimmer on his skin was the lights, the victory, or the screen. Now I suppose it was the cancer. The scar tissue. Not victory, exactly. The chaotic pop music in the surgeon's office. Asking for a different station just came out *Uhn*. The reconfiguring of priorities. The streamlining. The yoghurt. The words *corporate* and *cooperate* are not etymologically related. The majority. The procession of dignitaries. His body is in the coffin. The clips are from the past. You may taste garlic as the anaesthetic takes effect. The public outpouring. The holes in my head. People trusted him to do good things for them. To try, anyway. The impaction. The pinko fringe. The wisdom. The future. The full-on screed.

Can I have an apple? Who's that? Is he the one who died? What's he talking about? When is Mom coming home? Why is everyone all lined up to see the coffin if it's closed and you can't even see if he's really inside it? Who are the people outside? Why aren't they dressed up? What did Mom mean when she said you shouldn't overdo it with the pussy-cat? We don't have a cat. Was she joking? Was that a grown-up joke? Does your whole face hurt or just your mouth? 'Cause your whole face looks weird. What's "inspire"? Are there big holes in your mouth where the teeth were? Will your wisdom grow back bigger? How do you know when so many people come to a funeral? Is it for the people who have more love or just for people who are more famous? What's the difference between famous and love? How many people would come to my funeral? Can I have an apple? Is that his wife? Who's that? She looks like she's funny but she's not being funny now. I know this song. It's from *Shrek*. Why won't you tell me anything?

5:30 p.m. on a Thursday

Time for a bit of breath and beer
    while the night leans over
        and stumbles into the yard
    like a man having a stroke.

Squirrels whiplash
    around the compromised maples,
        chuckling nervously.
    The newspaper reports

we can now manufacture earthquakes.
    And yet here I am,
        inhabiting a space
    on the porch like a real man,

with all the concomitant benefits.
    The beer is cold and foamy,
        and even the non-recyclable
    cup bears a satisfying weight

as its sweat drips onto my lap.
    Burning nearby forests
        send delicious barbecue odours
    over the mountains.

Then, like a punch line, a crabapple
    drops into the plastic
        kiddie pool and drowns.

The Woman from Fire

To culminate our Festival we invited the Woman from Fire. She arrived at dawn, red-eyed and frazzled. Her hair was streaked, or perhaps singed. None of us had ever lived in Fire, though some had visited, but we resisted the urge to pepper her with questions – What was it like? What did people do to cope? The Woman from Fire asked for a scarf and frowned at the taste of our coffee. She seemed always on the verge of some startling revelation, and she flinched at any unexpected noise. She said, "Every day my blood boils and at night, while I sleep, it simmers." Then she lit a cigarette and blew smoke into her hands. How exciting it must be to live in Fire! How street-savvy every citizen! How could one live in Fire and not develop an essential understanding of mankind's inner essence? We introduced ourselves because we wanted to watch ourselves encounter her. The Woman from Fire sighed with annoyance or gratitude at our welcoming gestures and remarks, the burnt toast and euphemisms.

When it was her turn to present, the Woman from Fire stomped up to the platform and dismissed the dangling microphone. She spoke in a pained voice that rasped and cracked in all corners of our quaint sensibilities. Her language, it must be said, was unseemly, and her subjects were far from what we'd come to expect from the speakers at our Festival. But we are nothing if not an open-minded audience, and we responded warmly, feeling that we had become privy to something. We purchased books for our nightstands and thanked her in sincere fashion. She seemed distracted, or perhaps hungry. She admitted to us privately that she was happy to have a short vacation away from Fire. We returned her to her hotel room, where she lit a candle precariously close to the dust ruffle and spent the night scanning the channels for news from Fire, news none of us could tell her, news she already knew. In the morning, pink from her sauna, she raced to catch an early flight and left us to our imaginings and symposia.

We are a people of the air. We hold our Festivals. We attend our evenings. We speak in elaborate sentences that we admit tend toward a mandarin sadness. And yet, when we saw the Woman from Fire, there was something inside us – all of us – that reeled and struggled in a way that felt like burning. We *did* burn. There was smoke in our throats as we re-entered the world we know that surrounds and comforts us.

Yellow House Spider

clings by web and claw
to the shower tiles.

Naked, slick with soap,
I watch her try to

weather the crisis.
Everywhere I look

there are signs the world
wants to shake us loose.

The hot rain streams down.
What should I not do?

The Museum of Sound

On the ground floor, near the gift shop, is the Mechanical Wing, with sections for vehicles, factories, heavy equipment, and office machinery. A rare recording of FDR's typist is the prize of the Light Work Collection, but Vehicles are the bigger draw, with everything from a Model T to the Apollo 11 lunar module to a Sopwith Camel with a bullet pinging in the crankcase as it plummets toward the ground.

On the other side are the birdsong cubicles, organized by continent, with a special room for the extinct. The collection here is, regrettably, incomplete.

In the Talking Wing there are areas for Great Speeches (Hitler, Mandela), Lisps, Accents, Languages. Again, the prize pieces are the epics of the vanished.

Of course, it's the Music Wing that everyone comes for. The chance to hear Gershwin played by Gershwin, Beethoven played by Beethoven, Beethoven played by Gershwin, Gershwin played by Beethoven.

There are rumours about a Passion Collection, donated by a notorious Hollywood madam, but whatever exists has been sequestered.

Somewhere around here is a booth where you can test your aural spectrum. One woman swore she heard the keening of mating mosquitoes, but the Curators thought it unlikely. The human ear is ultimately a narrow instrument, like a bottle opener.

Come, let's explore the Hall of Winds. We can listen to a gale playing a sixteenth-century pipe organ in a bombed-out Croatian church. I will rub your neck in the storm.

Or let's go hear the howling on the moon.

ACKNOWLEDGEMENTS

Thanks to the editors of the following journals and magazines, in which many of these poems first appeared, some in radically different incarnations: *Adroit Journal*, *ARC*, *Cincinnati Review*, *Contemporary Verse 2*, *Event*, *Fiddlehead*, *Hamilton Stone Review*, *Joyland.com*, *Malahat Review*, *New Ohio Review*, *RiddleFence*, *The Walrus*.

"Dwarf" uses text from Alan Boyle's *The Case for Pluto* (John Wiley & Sons, 2010) and Chen Li's essay in the March 2010 issue of *Poetry* magazine. The epigraph is from a press conference that Ron Artest gave in September 2010. (He legally changed his name to Metta World Peace in September 2011.)

"Before the Conference Call" appeared in *Best Canadian Poetry, 2013*, edited by Molly Peacock and Sue Goyette (Tightrope Books, 2014).

"Security Camera" is for Alex Porco and the baristas at Toronto local Starbucks #4226.

"Wish You Were." Thanks to Puneet Kohli and Greg Payne for financial advice.

"Reading Drew Faust at the Outlet Mall" uses quotations (some from diaries and letters of Civil War soldiers) found in Drew Faust's fascinating *This Republic of Suffering* (Knopf, 2008).

"The Last Matador." Thanks to Elizabeth Ruth for bullfighting knowledge.

"We Oppose the Teaching of Higher Order Thinking Skills." The title is a quotation from the Texas Republican Party platform of 2012. The Bill Matthews poem I refer to is "The Blues," from his 1989 collection, *Blues If You Want*.

"Check Authenticity Here." The quotation about Weldon Kees is adapted from the Poetry Foundation's "Essential Poets" podcast series.

"We Are Here." Thanks to Michelle Shulman, Lisa Richler, Joanna Shapiro, and the rest of the moms in the pickup line at the Toronto Heschel School.

"Day's Work" is for Randy Cass and Col. Jason Brent.

"They Will Take My Island" was first published on, and was partly set in motion by, Paul Vermeersch's online project of that name. Thanks, Paul. See here: http://theywilltakemyisland.blogspot.ca

"Nearly Blank Calendar" uses text about washing bedridden patients from ehow.com. Thanks, more importantly, to Doctor Adrian Grek and Anne Marie Vico, from the Reitman Centre for Alzheimer's Support, for crucial insights.

"What I Know About Phenomenology." Thanks to Avishai Sol for clarifying some Pokémon terminology. The quoted lyric is from "Shadrach" on the Beastie Boys' *Paul's Boutique* (1989). Check it. This poem is for Ken Babstock.

"Poem for Noah Pozner": Noah Pozner was the youngest victim of the Sandy Hook Elementary School shootings in Newtown, Connecticut, on December 14, 2012. The text that closes the poem was taken from an interview his mother, Veronique Pozner, gave with Naomi Zeveloff.

"City Song" appeared in *The White Collar Book: Poetry and Prose of Canadian Business Life*, edited by Bruce Meyer, published by Black Moss Press, 2011.

"Ivory Fugue" uses text from a *National Geographic* article on the ivory trade written by Bryan Christy and published in October 2012. Thanks again to Puneet Kohli for information about Ganesh.

"Watching Jack Layton's Funeral" appeared in *Jack Layton: Art in Action*, edited by Penn Kemp and published by Quattro Books in 2013.

Thanks to the Banff Arts Centre for a residency during which some of this was crystallized, drafted, and daydreamed. Thanks to Laurentian University for giving my professorial self a home, for paying for things like Banff, and for giving me a sabbatical in order to finish. Thanks to John Degen for professional advice.

If writing a book of poems were like planting a garden, then I'd thank Kevin Connolly and Harold Heft for helping plant seeds; Ken Babstock, Vivé Griffith, and Karen Solie for rigorous hoeing and tending; and Dionne Brand for a master gardener's discerning eye when it came time to harvest. That would make Ellen Seligman, Lynn Henry, Anita Chong, and everyone at M&S and Random House of Canada the rain. Thanks would also go to my family for being the earth, my sons for being the bees, and Yael, of course, for being the sun.